PIDGIN
TO DA MAX

**Originally conceived, written and illustrated by Douglas Simonson (Peppo)
in collaboration with Ken Sakata and Pat Sasaki**

published by da Bess Press

T'ANKS, EH YOU GUYS!

Original layout and design, Paul Otaguro
Typesetting and photography, Graphic Prep Inc.

Bess Press
3565 Harding Avenue
Honolulu, Hawai'i 96816

BessPress.com

Printed in China

Reprinted 2021

INTRODUCTION
(Standard English)

PIDGIN TO DA MAX is for fun. We took a lot of pidgin words and put them down the way we use them, the way we hear them, and had fun with it. We hope you have fun with it, too.

We also want you to know that we have great reverence for pidgin, because in some ways it's like the heartbeat of Hawaii. When local people get together and relax, they talk pidgin. It comes from the heart.

Putting pidgin into written form wasn't easy. Probably you'll find things you would have written down differently. That's okay, because there are as many variations of pidgin as there are people. We did our best to make it as clear as possible—and the pictures help.

We hope no one is insulted by any of the definitions or cartoons in PIDGIN TO DA MAX. We don't want to insult anybody— but we kidded everybody!

We hope our love of Hawaii and of pidgin comes through, because that's why we put this book together—to give something back to the people, and the land, that have given so much to us.

> With much aloha,
> PEPPO
> KEN
> PAT

INTRODUCTION
(Pidgin)

'Ey! Dis book GOOD FUN, brah! 'Ass why we wen put 'um togeddah you know: so you guys could have good fun too!

But one noddah ting: we get special feeling about pidgin. 'Cause pidgin is special. Local people, dey get togeddah fo' party, wedding, baby luau, whatevahs, dey gotta talk story, yeah? An' how you can talk story wid'out pidgin? Cannot! Pidgin someting from da heart!

You know, we get hahd time fo' put da kine down on paper! An' garans ballbarans, you going look at some da words we get, you going say, "WOW! How dey came up wid' dat? Da guys lolo!" No beeg ting, brah. Mebbe you jus' from one noddah neighborhood! We only can try fo' put down da words people use da most . . . an' sometimes Waianae pidgin stay real diff'rent from Kaimuki pidgin, yeah? So you know, hang loose. Anyway, you gonna like da pictures.

An' you know, we no like insult any particular group of people in da islands—we jus' like kid everybody.

We love Hawaii, an' we love pidgin, an' dass da main ting we trying fo' say.

So kick back, bruddahs, an' relax wit' PIDGIN TO DA MAX!

> Aloha,
> PEPPO
> KEN
> PAT

A WORD OF CAUTION TO THE NON-LOCAL

If you don't already speak pidgin, you might need some help from local friends to understand this book. Remember, PIDGIN TO DA MAX is not a tourist guide to pidgin. So don't try to speak it after reading this book. You'll just get into trouble.

ACT (ak)
See NO ACT.

AKAMAI (AH kuh my)
Smart. Somebody
who really knows
the score.

ALL BUS' UP
(all bus UP) Destroyed.
"Junior's face all bus'
up from da fight!"
See also BUS' UP.

AKAMAI WAHINE

ALA-ALAS (all uh ALL uhz)
The family jewels.
"Wow, da guy when keeck
mah ALA-ALAS! Ah t'ought
da buggah going BUS'!"

ALA-ALAS

AN' DEN? (an DEN)
And then? So? So what else?
This can also mean "I'm bored."

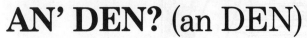

—AN' DEN?

ANY KINE (ENNY kine) Anything.
Haole: "She'll say anything to
get her way."
Pidgin: "She tell ANY KINE fo'
get her way."

HAWAIIAN BLUES SINGER

ASS WHY (ass WHY) That's the reason.
   Haole: "We can't afford it."
   Pidgin: "We no can affo'd 'um, ass why!"
ASS WHY HARD (ass why HAHD)
   Life is tough, yeah?

BACHAN (BAH chon) Buddahead popo. Also OBACHAN.

BAFE, BAVE (bayf, bayv) To take one bocha, o'one showah. "So, LeRoy, you going bafe o' wot?"

BAG To leave, to split. Also BAG IT.

HAOLE

PIDGIN

BAGGIES (BAG eez) Surfer shorts.
Good for showing off sweet okole.

BAGOONG
(bah gah ONG)
Fish sauce.
Filipino hum ha.

BAKATARE
(bah kah TAH deh)
Cuckoo. Lolo.

BAMBUCHA
(bom BOO cha) Big.
Also used to mean
certain parts of the
body, but only when
they're **big.**

BANANA (ba NA na)
Haolefied Oriental.

Yellow on the outside, white on the inside.

BEEF Fight. See also LIKE BEEF?

BEN Variation of WEN.
"I forgot." = "I ben forget."

BENJO (BEN jo)
Japanese word for LUA.
"Mits went benjo. Too much beers."

BENTO (BEN toe) Box lunch,
Japanese style.

BILOT (bee LOT) Filipina fufuna.

BLALA (BLAH lah)
The Moke's Moke.

BOBURA (BO boo dah) Japanese person born and raised in Japan who has the nerve to come to Hawaii.

BOCHA (BO cha) Bath. "Howcum you nevah take bocha yet?"

BODDAH YOU (bah duh YOU)
"What, you like start somet'ing?"
Also means "Get lost!"
Also: WHY, BODDAH YOU?

BOLOHEAD (BO lo hed) No mo' hair.

BORINQUE (bo DING kee) Puerto Rican.

BORO-BOROS

BORO-BOROS (bo do BO doze) The most had-it clothes you own. Worn for special occasions like painting the house, fixing the car, etc.

BOTO (BO toe) Manong chimpo.

BRAH (brah) Bruddah. "Howzit, brah?"

BREAK
Wave action.
BROK' (broke)
Here are some ways you can use BROK'.

1. Intense experience.

2. Broken or torn.

3. Break, bust.

BUDDAHEAD (BOO da hed)
Japanese person. Careful how you use this.

BUKBUK (F.O.B.)

BUGGAH (BUG ah)
1. Guy, friend. "Ey you buggahs!"
2. Pest. "Dat buggah try anyt'ing, I slap hees head!"

BUKBUK (BOOK-BOOK) Manong.

BULAI (boo LIE) Lies.
"Ey, no bulai, brah!"

BUMBYE, BAMBAI (bum BYE) Soon enough. This is the most exact measurement of time in pidgin. "Bumbye we going ovah Harold's, get radical!"

BUMMAHS (BUM ahz) Expression of disappointment or regret. Good for all kinds of occasions.

BUS' UP (bus UP) To broke. "Kalani wen BUS' UP da guy!"

BUT Though; however. Used at the end of a sentence. "Junior nice guy. He get ugly face but."

CANNOT Cannot.
  "You can go out
  tonight?" "Cannot!"
  Also pronounced
  CANNAH.
  "What—you cannah
  come?" See also
  NO CAN.

MY MODDAH SAY I
CANNAH GO OUT WIT'CHOO
TONIGHT, RODNEY! SHE
WEN SPAHK ALL DA
HICKEYS FROM LAS' TIME!

CATCH ME UP, CATCH YOU UP
  To overtake. "His cah too fas'! I
  nevah going catch heem up!"

CHAWAN CUT

CHAWAN CUT

(CHA won cut) Like one upside-down bowl on top yo' head.

CHEE (cheeee) This expression has many uses. Here are just a few:

DISAPPOINTMENT

CHEE CHAHLENE—WHY YOU NO LIKE LET ME TOUCH YOU?

FRUSTRATION

CHEE! LATERS FO' CHAHLENE! SHE NEVAH LET ME DO NOTTING!

DELIGHT

CHEE, CHAHLENE—YOU TAHREEFIC!

DISGUST

CHEE! DAT CHAHLENE! SHE LET YOU DO ANY KINE, YEAH?

CHICKEN SKIN (CHEE ken skeen) What you get on your skin when you get chills. Variation of STAND-UP HAIRS. "When we wen keess, ah got CHICKEN SKIN!"

CHIMPO (CHEEM po) Boy's da kine.
CHING-CHING Pilau pake word.

CHO-CHO LIPS

CHO-CHO LIPS
(CHO cho lips)
Thick lips.

CHOP SUEY
Kapakahi;
all mixed up.

CHOP SUEY

COASTING
(KOAS teen)
1. Not busy.
2. What you do on weekends when you no mo' date.
3. Unemployed.

4. The state between relaxation and unconsciousness. Also: COAST'UM: Never mind; forget it.

COCKAROACH
(KA ka roach) To steal or sneak away with. Also tight or stingy.

COME

COME To become, to get.

COOL HEAD MAIN TING No big deal. Relax already.

CRACK SEED Pake munchies.

DA 1. The.

Haole: "The young girl placed her foot on the brick."

Pidgin: "Da cheeck wen keeck da breeck."

2. How.

Haole: "How cute!"

Pidgin: "Oh, da cute!"

3. So.

Haole: "It's so hot!"

Pidgin: "Oh, da hot!"

DA KINE (da KINE) Da kine is the keystone of pidgin. You can use it anywhere, anytime, anyhow. Very convenient. What would we do without DA KINE? "'Ey, I no can da kine if you no like da kine too!"

DAIKON LEGS (DYE kon legs) Legs like daikon—fat, short and white.

DAT That. "Dat ugly guy yo' boyfrien'?" See also LI'DAT.

-DEM Them. You can add this word on when you want to describe a whole bunch of people and you don't want to name them all. Also -GUYS, -FOLKS.

DOO ITASHIMASHITE (don't touch my MUS tache) You're welcome.

DRILLED Adjective describing the condition of a surfer or bodysurfer who has unsuccessfully negotiated a killer wave. "Wow, man, I got drilled at Makapuu today!"

EASY

EASY (EE zee)
Take it easy.
"Easy, brah!"

EH? You know?
You understand?
Pidgin for "NE?"

EHU (EH hoo) Red-headed Hawaiian.

'EM (um) See 'UM.

ETE (EH teh)
Somebody who lacks the most basic social skills. Someone who just doesn't know how to fit in is considered "ETE".

EVERY TIME. All the time; always.
Haole: "He's always making a fool of himself."
Pidgin: "He go make ass every time".

'EY! (ay!) Hey! Hey you, wake up! This is an attention-getter.

FA'A FAFINE (fa ah fa FEE neh) (also fa fa FEENG geh) Samoan mahu.

FLIP Bukbuk, Manong.

F.O.B. Fresh Off the Boat. This applies to any non-haole immigrant still wearing the same hairstyle and clothes they wore back home. Also J.O.J.: Just Off the Jet.

F.O.B

TO (Haole)

FO' (Pidgin)

FOR, FO' (FOAH) To.

Haole: "I was only trying to get to know you."

Pidgin: "Ah was on'y tryeen fo' touch yo' body."

FOR WHAT?/FOR WHY? Why?

"Fo' what you came ovah heah, turkey?"

FOR DAYS (fo' DAZE) Plenty, a lot.

Haole: "He certainly has long hair."

Pidgin: "He get hair fo' DAYS!"

FO' REAL (fo' REEL) This expression can mean several things. For instance:

1. ALARM. "You kidding me?"

2. AGREE-MENT. "You can say that again!"

3. THREAT. "I'm not kidding, buster!"

FROM BEFORE Before.

FROM LONG TIME Long time.
   Haole: "I've known her for quite a while."
   Pidgin: "I know her from long time."

FROM NOW Now.

FRUIT PUNCH
(froo' PUNCH)
The State Drink
   of Hawaii.
Goes well with
   PLATE LUNCH.

FUFUNA
(foo FOO nah)
Samoan or
Tongan lady's
da kine. (USE
WITH CAUTION.)

FROM NOW

FUNNY KINE (FUN nee kine)
Strange, different. "Oh, he ac' real
FUNNY KINE!"

FUT

FUT
How you spell
"relief" in pidgin.

FUTLESS
Frustrated;
confused; spaced
out. If the Rolling
Stones came from
Waipahu, "I Can't
Get No Satisfaction"
would have been
"Chee! I Stay
All Futless!"

GARANS (GAYR unz) Guaranteed. For sure. "Garans, brah!"

Also GARANS BALLBARANS (gayr unz ball BEAR unz).

GECKO (GEH ko)
Local lizard. Good
luck to have inside
your house.

GEEV'UM (GEEVum)
Go for it! Give it all
you got!

GECKO ORDERING

GET Have.
Haole:
"I have a cold."
Pidgin:
"I get one cold."

GET

GET CHANCE? "I like fool aroun' wit'choo!"

GO, GOING (GO, GO een) Pidgin future tense.

Haole: "I think I'll make some soup."

Pidgin: "Bimeby I goeen mek saimin."

GOOD FUN In Pidgin, FUN is okay, but GOOD FUN is better. "How da pahty was?" "Oh, was GOOD FUN!"

GOOFY FOOT Surfer who puts his right foot forward.

GRIND (GRINE) To eat.

GRINDS (GRINES) Food. "Ovah deah, get plenny grinds fo' da money."

GRIND

-GUYS See -DEM.

HAD-IT. Wasted, destroyed, wrecked.
Haole: "Boy, am I tired."
Pidgin: "Wow, I real HAD-IT!"

HAAAH? Pidgin for "Sorry, I didn't hear you."

HANA HOU (ha na HO). Do it again. Instant replay. One mo' time!

HANABATA (ha na BAH ta) What you gotta wipe when yo' nose come runny.

HANAI (ha NYE) Adopted.

HANAKOKOLELE (ha na ko ko LEH Leh) Shame on you! Also AHANAKOKOLELE.

WHEAH WE GET HANABATA.

HANAKUSO (ha na KOO so)
Hahd kine hanabata.

HANDLE (HAN doh) To maintain.
"Oh, wow, man, I too loaded!
I cannot HANDLE!"

HAOLE

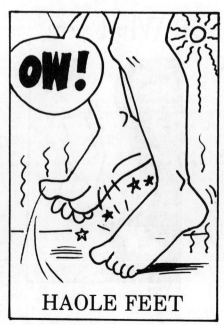

HAOLE FEET

HAOLE (HOW lee)
Caucasian, or someone
who acts like one.
"Marie real nice,
but her seestah so
HAOLE!"

HAOLE FEET
Tender tootsies.

HAOLEFIED (HOW lee fide) Just like a haole. "George went mainlan' and' he wen come back so haolefied I hahdly knew heem!"

HAPAI (ha PIE) Knocked up.

HAUNA (HOW nah) Stink.

HAUNA

HAWAIIAN TIME Late.

HEAH (HEE ah) Here. Not there (DEAH). Also OVAH HEAH; OVAH DEAH.

HELE ON (Heh leh ON) To get moving.

HEMAJANG (HEH muh jang) All mix up; kapakahi.

HEMO (HEM oh) To take off or remove. "Hemo yo' shoes when you eenside da house!" Hemo skin = Peeling.

HOLOHOLO (ho lo HO lo) To go out. "You like go holoholo tonight?"

HONEST KINE (ON nus kine) Fo' real? You mean it?

HORRAHS (HAW ruz) Bad, terrible.

HOWZIT (HOW zit) Pidgin for "aloha".

HUHU (HOO hoo) To be upset.
  Haole: "Relax. Don't get upset."
  Pidgin: "No huhu, brah."

HULI (HOO lee) To turn over; to flip. "Wow, da cah was goeen so fas', da buggah wen HULI!"

HUM HA (hum HA) Pake bagoong.

HUMBUG

HUMBUG (HUM bug, hum BUG) Bother, hassle. "Real humbug fo' do all dees ovah, you know!"

HYBOLIC (hi BAH lik) To talk like one intellectual-kine haole.

I OWE YOU MONEY O' WOT?
Pidgin for "How come you staring at me?"

ICE SHAVE This is how they say "shave ice" on the Big Island.

INNAHS (EE nahs) The thing to do. Great, hot, righteous. "Wow, da surf so INNAHS today!"

INSIDE (een SIDE) In, into.
Haole: "Put two potatoes in the salad."
Pidgin: "Try put two potatoes eenside da salad."

JUICE Rigged.
"Dees one JUICE GAME, man!"
Big, powerful surf. "Big sets today!
Lotta JUICE!"

JUNK Lousy, terrible. "Wow, what a junk movie!"

JUNKS 1. What girls carry in their purses. 2. What guys carry in their car trunks.
See also STUFFS.

JUNKS

KALUA PIG (kah loo ah PEEG) This is what you get when you put the pua'a inside the imu and let 'em cook.

KAKI'O (ka KEE oh) Scab.

'KAY DEN!

KAPAKAHI (kah puh KAI) All mix up; all mess up.

KAUKAU (COW cow) 1. Grinds. 2. To grind.

KAY DEN (KAY den) Okay then! All right already!

KEAO (kay OW) Samoan for KUKAE.

KEFE (KEH feh) Pilau Samoan word. Don't even THINK this word in front of a Samoan. Also TEFE.

KIM CHEE Korean mouthwash neutralizer.

KOTONK (kuh TONK) Japanese person from the U.S. mainland. Hollow-head buddahead.

KUKAE (koo KAI) What the neighborhood dogs deposit on your lawn if you don't put out the water jars.

KULEANA (koo lee AH Nah) Responsibility, job. "I no like do dat— da garbage yo' kuleana!"

KUMU (koo moo) 1. Teacher. 2. Lover. (If you lucky, you get both at da same time!)

LAKAS ((LAH kahz) Hawaiian for "loins". Used freely—among certain segments of the population. "Wow, he get plenny lakas!"

LAYDAHS, LEDDAHS (LAY duz, LEH duz) Later.
1. See you later. "Leddahs, uh, John?"
2. I've had it. "Laydahs fo' HEEM!"

LAYDAHS

LAU LAU (rhymes with POW) Individually wrapped servings of meat and fish, Hawaiian style.

LEFTS (LEFS) Waves breaking to the left. See also RIGHTS.

LEPO (LEH po) 1. Filthy 2. Loser; screw-up; always make ass. See also MOE LEPO, PILAU.

LI'DAT

LI'DAT
(lah DAT) Like that. Used to explain something you don't want to bother explaining.

LIKE To want or want to. HAOLE:"May I have the pleasure of this dance?" PIDGIN: "You like dance?"

LIKE BEEF?
Invitation to go outside.

LIMU
(LEE moo) Seaweed. Good fo' eat.

See also OGO.

GRADUATION DAY

GOOD PARTY

LOCAL STYLE

LOCAL STYLE Anything typical of the way people do things in Hawaii.

LOLO (LO lo) Someone who would be glad to give you the time of day—if he knew how to read a clock.

LOMI (LO mee) Rub, massage. I went up Tant'lus las' night wit' Cheryl—she wen geev me da BIG LOMI!"

LOMPAI (loam PIE) 1. To bother. "Ey, no lompai, brah!" 2. Good for nothing. "Oh, you so LOMPAI!"

LUAU FEET

LUA (LOO ah) Hawaiian benjo. "Mits went lua. Too much beers."

LUAU FEET (LOO ow feet) Big feet.

LUA

MAHALO

MAHALO

(ma HA lo)

Tourist-ese for "T'anks eh?" Used mostly by entertainers, aunties, and inter-island flight attendants.

MAHU (MA hoo)
1. Guys who like fool around with guys. 2. Drag queen. "No mess aroun' wit dose mahus down Hotel Shtreet, brah! Dose buggahs radical!"

MAHU

MAKAI (ma KAI) Opposite of MAUKA.

MAKE (MOCK ay) Dead.

MAKE-DIE-DEAD (mock ay die DED) Really dead.

MAKE "A" (mek AY) Make ass.

MAKE ASS

MAKE ASS (mek ASS) To screw up; to make a fool of yourself. See NO MAKE ASS.

MAKULE (mah KOO leh) Old. "Ey, getteen makule, eh, brah?"

MALASADA (mah lah SAH da) Portuguese donut. No hole.

MANE'O (ma NAY oh) Turned on. "No touch me deah, I going come MANE'O!"

MANINI (ma NEE nee) 1. Stingy. (See MANJU, COCKAROACH) 2. Undersized. "Oh, he get one manini one!"

MANJU (MON Joo) Tight. See MANINI, COCKAROACH.

MANONG (muh NONG) Filipino. See also P.I., BUK-BUK, FLIP.

MAUKA (MAU ka) Opposite of MAKAI.

MAX Maximum. "To da max" means "All the way."

MAX OUT To overdo it. To da max, and then some.

MAX OUT

MINES

MINES Mine. "Yawz stay mo' small den mines!"

MINORS (MY nuz) No big thing. "But I no mo' money fo' da movies!" "Minors, brah. I get."

MOE LEPO (mo eh LEH po) Expression of disgust meaning REALLY PILAU. Wrinkle up your nose when you say this. Also M'LEPO.

MOEMOE (mo ay MO ay) Sleep.

MOKE (moke)
Local boy whose idea of a good time is to broke some body's face. Male counterpart of TITA.

MOMONA (mo MO na) Fat.

MO' (mo) More.
  Haole: "He is fatter than I am."
  Pidgin: "He mo' fat dan me!"

MO' BETTAH (mo BEH dah) Better.

MUSHY 1. Sloppy waves. 2. Sloppy
  rice.

MUSUBI (moo soo BEE) Rice balls.
  Get ume inside.

MO' BETTAH

NAH NAH NAH NAH NAH (Nah nah nah nah NAH) Just kidding.

NAILS The pits. Not making it. "Wow, da prom was NAILS dees year!"

NENE (NAY nay) 1. Sleep (Japanese) 2. Goose (Hawaiian)

Haole: "The goose is asleep." Pidgin: "Da nene stay nene."

NERJUS (NER jus) Nervous.

NI'ELE (nee EH leh) Nosy.

NI'ELE

NO ACT (No AK)
Stop showing off. Cool it.

NO CAN
(no CAN)
Cannot.

NO MAKE ASS
(no mek ASS)
Don't make a
fool of yourself.

NO ACT

NO CAN

NO MAKE FUN

NO MAKE FUN (no mek FUN) Don't tease.

NO MAKE LI'DAT (no mek lah DAT) Don't act like that.

NO MENTION (no MEN chun) You're welcome. Don't mention it.

NO MO'
(no MOAH)
None.
Haole:
"I have
no money."
Pidgin:
"I no mo'
kala."

NO MO' CLASS No class at all.

NO MO' NOTTING
(no moah NAWteeng)
Nothing.
"Wow, fishing was
JUNK yestidday.
No mo' NOTTING!"

NO MO' NOBODY Nobody.

NO NEED Unnecessary. "Want me to bring some pupus?" "No need."

NO SHAME 1. Don't be shy. "Come on out, Bobby. No shame!" 2. Wow, doesn't anything embarrass you? "Wow, Elmer, no shame!"

NO SHAME

NO TALK STINK (no talk STEENK)
Don't say nasty things behind people's backs.

NOT!/NO TALK STINK

NOT! You gotta be kidding! No can be!

OF This word is easy to use in pidgin. Just drop it.

Haole: "I have three of these, so how many of these do I have?"

Pidgin: "I get t'ree da kine, so how many da kine I get?"

OGO (OH go) Limu

OKOLE (oh KO leh) What you sit on in Hawaii. This word does not mean 'barstool.'

I LIKE POPOLO BOYS, YOU KNOW, BUT DEAH OKOLES SO BAMBUCHA!

OKOLE

ONREAL (ahn REEL) Unreal. Used to describe anything that gets your motor going, like somebody sexy, dynamite dope, or big waves. "Wow, unreal da sets, yeah?"

OPIHI (oh PEE hee) Screwdriver on the rocks.

OPIHI

OR WHAT? (o WOT) Add this phrase to a question to give it that local feeling.
Haole: "Do you want to eat?"
Pidgin: "So, you like eat o' wot?"

ON TOP On.
Haole: "I spilled it on my shirt."
Pidgin: "I wen spill 'um on top mah shirt!"

ONE "A." Haole: "Do you have a car?"
Pidgin: "You get one cah?"

ONE NODDAH (won NAW duh)
One more. Another. "Wait, I get one noddah t'ing fo' tell you!"

ONO (OH no)
Delicious. "Wow, ONO da malasadas, yeah?" Also ONOLICIOUS.

ONO/ONE NODDAH

P.I. (pee EYE) Manong (usually F.O.B.).

PAKALOLO (pah ka LO lo) Dees
 word mean . . . oh, wow, I no can
 remembah . . . try wait, I tryeen fo'
 t'ink . . . oh wow . . .

WOW, WILSON! YOU WAS GONE LONG TIME!

BRUCE SO PAKE! HEES TOILET PEP-PAH DISPEN-SAH ONLY GEEV ONE SQUARE AT A TIME!

PAKE (pah KAY)
Chinese. Nevah
like spend money.

PAKE

PAU (pow) Over, done, through. "Put 'em away when you pau."

PAU HANA (pow HA na) Pau work.

PEPPAH (PEH pah) Paper.

PAU HANA

PEPPAH

PILAU

PILAU (Pee LAU) Filthy; dirty. "Go wash, Bertram! Yo' hands so PILAU!"

PLATE LUNCH State food of Hawaii.

PLENTY (PLEN nee) Lots. "Chee, get plenny peoples heah!"

POI DOGS

POCHO (PO cho) Portuguese.

POI DOG Local mixture.

POPO (PO po) Pake tutu.

POPOLO (po PO lo) Local boy—from Harlem.

PORTUGUESE (PO da ghee) Local people skilled in the art of endless conversation.

PORTAGEE JOKES

Disgusting example of ethnic prejudice.

"What's black and crispy and hangs from a light fixture?"

"I donno."

"A portagee electrician!"

PRESSURE OUT (preh shah OUT)
To go to pieces because you cannot handle. "Ey, no tell Lance about hees girlfrien', brah—he going PRESSURE OUT!"

PUKA (POO kah) Swiss cheese get plenny dese. "Ey, you get pukas eenside yo' head o' wot?"

PUMPING

PUMPING (PUM peen) Going strong. Good action.

PUPUS

PUPUS (POO pooz) Local hors
  d'oeuvres. "What kine pahty dees?
  No mo' pupus!"

RADICAL (RAD ee koh) Heavy duty.
Extreme. Pushing it to da max.

RADICAL

RADICAL OUT (rad ee koh OUT) So radical it's **more** than radical. "Las' time I wen smoke Alan's homegrown, I wen RADICAL OUT!"

RIGHTS Waves breaking right. "How da rights?" See also LEFTS.

RIPPER, RIPPAH
Somebody who really tears it up.

RIPPER

SAIMIN (sai MIN) When nothing else looks good, there's always saimin. "I cannot decide what I like eat . . . gimme saimin."

SASHIMI (sa SHEEmee) Raw fish. Good with shoyu and mustard and beer.

SASHIMI

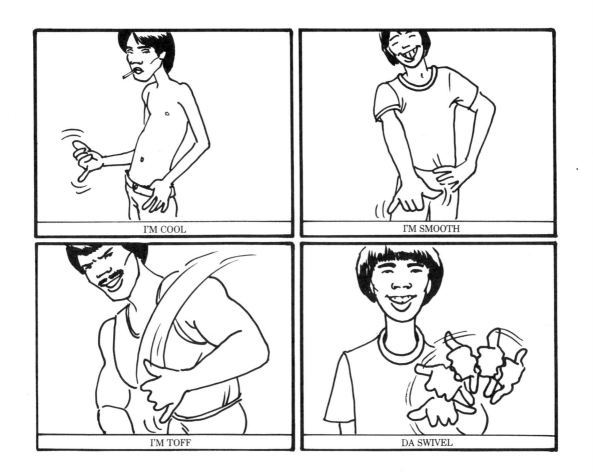

I'M COOL

I'M SMOOTH

I'M TOFF

DA SWIVEL

SET A bunch of waves.

SHAKA (SHAH ka) 1. Right on!
2. Righteous! "Dat was some
SHAKA WEED, brah!" 3. Hand
signal meaning "Howzit?" and
various other things. (See
illustrations)

SHIBAI

SHAVE ICE Popular treat. Haoles call them SNO-CONES. See also ICE SHAVE.

SHIBAI (shee BUY) Bulai. B.S.

SHISHI (SHEE shee) What you do eenside da lua.

SHOYU (SHOI yu) What haoles put on rice.

SHTREET Street.

SIDE Area. Haole: "He lives near Waianae." Pidgin: "He stay Waianae side."

SIDE BOLOS (side BO lohz) 1. Drastic haircut. (See also BOLOHEAD) 2. Card game score when you really wipe out the other guy.

S'KEBEI (Skeh BAY, SKEH beh) 1. Dirty old man. 2. Mane'o. "S'kebei, you! No come neah me!"

S'KOSHI
(SKO shee)
Little bit.
Also S'KOSH.

SLACK KEY
Guitars on da mainland get tight strings. Island strings little bit mo' **relaxed.**

SLY MONGOOSE One clevah buggah.

SMALL-KID TIME

SMALL-KID TIME Hanabata days.

SOME GOOD Really good.

SOME ONO Really ono.

SOME PLENTY Lots. (Also used with good, ono, etc. "Some plenty ono, yeah?")

SPARK (spahk) To see; to check out. " 'Ey brah, you wen spahk da wahine get da beeg da kines?"

STAY

To be. If Hamlet had come from Waimanalo, he probably would have started his big speech a little differently.

STICK (steek) "surfboard"

STILL YET This can mean "still," "yet," or "but." "We can go pahty yo' house?" "Yeah, but my moddah stay wait up fo' me still yet."

STINK-EYE Dirty look. "Wow, you saw da stink-eye she wen geev me?"

STINKFISH Cuttlefish. You don't eat this before a date.

SUCK ROCKS

STUFFS Stuff. "Wow, get plenny stuffs eenside heah, yeah?" See also JUNKS.

SUCK WIND/SUCK ROCKS Stick it! Bug off! Get lost! (Also POUND SAND.)

SUSHI (SOO shee) Japanese pupu.

TALK STORY (talk STAH ree) Talk, gossip, shoot the breeze. "Siddown, relax, talk story wit' me."

TALKING STORY

T'ANKS EH?

TALOFA (ta LO fa) Samoan for
HOWZIT.

T'ANKS EH? Pidgin for MAHALO.

TELL To say.

Haole: "My mother's going to say I can't go."

Pidgin: "My muddah going tell, you no can go!"

T'INK SO

T'INK SO (tink SO) Think.

Haole: "You think it's going to rain today?"

Pidgin: "You t'ink so going rain today?"

TITA

TITA (TEE dah) Mokette. A local girl with a "special quality" —it's in the mouth.

TO DA MAX (to da MAX) All the way. One hundred percent.

TRY (try, chai, chry) Halfway between PLEASE and nothing at all.
POLITE: "Please come."
SEMI-POLITE: "Try come."
RUDE: "COME!"

TRYING

TRYING Pidgin for "You're trying too hard!"

TUTU (TOO too) Hawaiian popo. Plenny poi undah da bridge.

UFA (OO fa) Short for UFAMEA. You can use it as a verb or a noun, and it will probably get you into trouble either way.

UFAMEA
(oo fa MAY ah)
Samoan insult.
And you know
better than to
insult a Samoan.

UFA

UKUS (OO kooz) Itchy, yeah, dose little buggahs? Try use A-200 or Kwell.

UJI (OO jee) Expression of disgust. Used for everything from smelly garbage to somebody you can't stand.

ULE (OO leh) Boy's da kine. Hawaiian boto.

'UM, 'EM (um, em) Pidgin stay simple, you know. 'UM is pidgin singular **and** plural.

UME (OO meh) Plum. Get inside musubi.

UNREAL (See ONREAL.

USEDTATO

USEDTATO (USED ta to) Used to. Haole: I've grown accustomed to your face . . . "
Pidgin: "I getteen usedtato yo' face . . . "

WAHA (WAH ha) Talk too much.

WAHINE (wa HEE nay) Girl or woman.

WALA'AU (va la OW) Diarrhea of the mouth.

WALA'AU

WE GO Pidgin for "Let's split." See also BAG.

WEET'/WEED' With.

WEN This is pidgin automatic past tense.
Haole: "Did you see him?"
Pidgin: "You wen spahk da guy?"

WEED'/WEET'

WHA'S DA HAPS
(whass da HAPS)
What's happening?
What's new?

WHAT, WOT
1. "You like staht somet'ing?" Often used with LIKE BEEF or BODDAH YOU. "What–like beef?"

2. Attention-getter. Used before a question.

WHATEVAHS (what EV ahz) Very handy word. Can be used to mean almost anything. For instance:

"I don't want to talk about it."

"I don't know/ It doesn't matter."

"I'm just lolo over you."

WODDASCOOPS (wha da SCOOPS) What's happening? What's da happs? (Big Island use)

WOP YO'JAW This is something you say to someone when you've really got 'em on something. Also WOP IT, or WOP IT DOWN TO HEAH.

WOP YO' JAW

YEAH? You can put "yeah" in just about anywhere the rhythm feels right, or to make sure the other person is listening.

YEAH?

YEAH YEAH YEAH YEAH YEAH Yeah.

YOBO (YO bo) Seoul Bruddah.

YOU This is another attention-getter. When you put it at the end of a phrase it means "Yeah, you da one I talking to!" "No laugh, you!"

ZORIS (ZO ree) Sleepahs.

ZORIS